The ONE
YEAR
BIBLE

GOD SIGHTINGS™
LEARNING TO EXPERIENCE GOD EVERY DAY™

COMPANION GUIDE

Group

Loveland, Colorado
group.com

Group resources actually work!

This Group resource incorporates our R.E.A.L. approach to ministry. It reinforces a growing friendship with Jesus, encourages long-term learning, and results in life transformation, because it's

Relational
Learner-to-learner interaction enhances learning and builds Christian friendships.

Experiential
What learners experience through discussion and action sticks with them up to 9 times longer than what they simply hear or read.

Applicable
The aim of Christian education is to equip learners to be both hearers and doers of God's Word.

Learner-based
Learners understand and retain more when the learning process takes into consideration how they learn best.

GOD SIGHTINGS™
Learning to Experience God Every Day™

THE ONE YEAR COMPANION GUIDE

Copyright © 2009 Group Publishing, Inc.

Visit our website: **group.com**

Credits
Contributing Authors: Stephanie Caro, Bob D'Ambrosio, Kates S. Holburn, Mikal Keefer, Jan Kershner, Kristi Rector, Siv M. Ricketts, Larry Shallenberger, Carl Simmons, Kelli B. Trujillo, Amber Van Schooneveld, Vicki L.O. Witte, Jill Wuellner
Senior Editor: Candace McMahan
Chief Creative Officer: Joani Schultz
Art Director: Paul Povolni
Cover Designer: Holly Voget
Book Designers: Holly Voget and Jean Bruns
Print Production: Paragon Prepress
Production Manager: Peggy Naylor

ISBN: 978-0-7644-3925-4

10 9 8 7 6 5 4 3 2 1   18 17 16 15 14 13 12 11 10 09

Printed in the United States of America.

Welcome to God Sightings™

Once you've seen God at work, there's no turning back...

Not to a ho-hum, lukewarm faith. Not to a casual commitment to Christ. You're hooked—and likely to stay that way.

You're excited. Inspired. Open to the unexpected.

You can't wait to see what God will do next. Because—maybe for the first time—you see him *alive and active* in your world.

God hasn't retired, you know.

He's as busy now as he's ever been.

But until you see that with your own eyes, it's tough to have a vibrant faith. Believing in God can feel dry. Dusty. Grounded in principles rather than passion.

God Sightings™ changes everything.

Each week, as you make your way through God Sightings, you'll explore a Bible truth. Let it sink deep in your heart—and rise high in your expectations. Look for practical ways God is expressing that truth in the world around you, in your own life.

You'll pray. Jot observations in this journal. And be amazed.

Why? Because *you'll actually see God at work*. Not because he's suddenly shown up, but because you finally have eyes to see…and at last you're looking.

Fuel your faith.

It's one thing to master the Bible—to know about God and his history with his creation. It's great information, a rock-solid foundation.

But to *experience* God in a fresh, powerful way?

That's life itself.

God Sightings provides a focus too often missing in Bible study: looking past the pages to God himself. Discovering the Author, not just the literature.

So get ready. You're about to grow as you've never grown before.

Cement your faith.

If you've ever wondered—even for a moment—if God is real, or if he's truly engaged in your daily life, you're about to get your answer.

You'll soon know with certainty that you're not alone. You're not forgotten. You're seen, heard, and loved by the Creator of the universe—who knows your name as certainly as he knows when a sparrow falls to the ground or a lily springs up in a summer field.

So get ready. Your faith is about to become the bedrock of your life.

Witness your faith.

Jesus asked his followers not to become studied theologians or powerful debaters. He asked them to be *witnesses*—people willing to share their experiences.

He asks the same of you…and through God Sightings you'll quickly discover you have something to share. You'll be prepared to share stories of God's presence and power. His love in your life.

So get ready. Soon you'll be a witness to something so profoundly simple and powerful it changes lives: God's expressed love.

Jump right in.

Dive in on your own, or with a small group. Move at your own pace, or move through this book in one year. There are 52 sessions, but there's no reason to rush.

What matters isn't how fast you finish, but what happens along the way.

Get ready. You're on the journey of a lifetime.

And you'll never be the same.

God Sightings

This week, look for beginnings. For new life. Fresh starts. Clean slates. You'll see them everywhere. And each beginning is an echo of God's creative work in the world—a God Sighting.

God's a *big* fan of beginnings. He created a sprawling universe—a hotbed of beginnings—and then kept rolling. Kept crafting new starts and a new life… including yours.

So keep track of new beginnings this week. See them… celebrate them…jot a list here in your journal. Catch God at work.

Reflection Questions

If God is speaking to you, how would you describe God's "voice"? Why do you think God sounds that way to you?

How have you seen God work in other ways this week?

What are you waiting to hear from God about right now? Imagine waking up tomorrow morning to find God had miraculously solved your problem. What do you think God's solution would be?

∾Week 1—January 1-7

Genesis 1:1–18:15; Matthew 1:1–6:24;
Psalms 1–7; Proverbs 1:1–2:5

More God Sightings & *Prayers*

What else has God shown you this week? What do you think God wants you to do about it? Write it down. Draw it. Do it!

"My plan was to read the Bible all the way through, gathering evidence to prove once and for all that God did not really care about me. In the very first book of the Bible, I was stunned to read the story of Hagar... As God did with Hagar, he heard my anguished cry and saw my pain and suffering. With this realization, my eyes were opened to all the things God had done for me! I went down on my knees, crying and praying for forgiveness."

—Peggy Ann Kennedy, writer *

God Sightings

This week, look for how God is keeping his promises to you. Each promise kept is another reminder that God is—and that he's with you. It's a God Sighting.

God promised Isaac a long string of descendents, something that didn't happen during Isaac's lifetime. God keeps his own timeline…and it may not be yours. But while God won't be rushed, he *is* faithful.

What has God promised you?

List those promises here in your journal. Meditate on them. Thank God for doing what he says he'll do…in your lifetime—or beyond.

Reflection Questions

God spoke specifically and audibly to Abraham and to Isaac. Though you likely didn't have *that* experience, how *did* God communicate to you this past week? Which specific words from Scripture stood out most to you in your reading?

How else did God show up in your week? Describe a moment when you zeroed in on his presence.

The brilliant night sky was a symbol to Abraham and then to Isaac of God's promise. Think of something from your past week that can symbolize how you saw God at work in your life—anything from a simple object to something extravagant. Describe the symbol and what it means to you here.

❧Week 2—January 8–14

Genesis 18:16–31:16; Matthew 6:25–10:23;
Psalms 8–12; Proverbs 2:6–3:15

More God Sightings & Prayers

God is speaking to you. God is moving and at work in your world. But there may be weeks when, try as you might, it seems you just can't "hear" him or "see" him. Take a moment to think about the circumstances, doubts, stresses, or fears that may prevent you from really seeing God at work in your everyday life. List as many as you can think of here. Then cross them out, one by one, as you ask God to help you overcome them and to direct you in actions you can take to remove those roadblocks.

God Sightings

This week, look for ways God gives you rest. Times he helps you reboot and relax. Each of those moments is more than a breather—it's a God Sighting.

God understands that you're busy, that there are people who depend on you and deadlines with your name on them. But he also understands that you need to rest. And to rest in *him*.

This week, take note of where you find refreshing rest in your life. Capture your thoughts here in your journal.

Thank God for moments when it's not just your body that's refreshed…but your soul, too.

Reflection Questions

As you read God's Word, God reveals more and mor about himself to you. What specific traits of God's character has he emphasized to you in Scripture this past week?

What's a specific way you sensed Jesus inviting you to draw near to him this week? Was it through the kind words from a Christian friend? the words of a song? a peaceful breeze and a moment to breathe? Jo down *how* Jesus invited you…and how you responde to the invitation.

Imagine you could go back in time and take a photograph of a specific moment when you really saw God at work or sensed his presence this past week. What moment would you pick? What would the image portray?

❧Week 3—January 15-21

Genesis 31:17–43:34; Matthew 10:24–14:12;
Psalms 13:1–18:36; Proverbs 3:16–4:10

More God Sightings & Prayers

How else has God interrupted the busyness of your life this week to draw your focus from the hectic to the eternal? How do you feel God nudging you…pointing you…directing you…convicting you…pushing you…to act?

"One morning…after my mother's death, a new wave of grief swept over me, and I felt especially burdened about the fact that no one had been with my mother at the moment of her death. In the midst of my despair, God reminded me of Genesis 28:16, in which Jacob…came to realize that God may very well be present and working even when our human senses are not aware of him. I cannot express the comfort I felt in reading that verse."

—Anna DeRosa*

God Sightings

If the Lord is your shepherd, what does that make you?

A sheep. A small, defenseless mammal facing life without claws, without self-control, and without a clue. Plus, sheep are remarkably tasty.

In the same way a sheep needs a shepherd, you need guidance. Direction. Encouragement. A clue.

This week, pay attention to where you get guidance. Realize that whenever you receive good advice, it's God speaking into your life. It's a God Sighting.

Jot down what you hear…and what you do in response.

Reflection Questions

In all you read from different parts of Scripture this past week, what common themes stood out to you?

How has God reassured you of his active presence in your life this week?

Imagine you were writing a book about your life and your relationship with God. If this past week were a chapter in that book, what would the title be? What would you focus on?

❧ WEEK 4—January 22-28

Genesis 44:1–Exodus 7:25; Matthew 14:13–19:12;
Psalms 18:37–23:6; Proverbs 4:11–5:23

More God Sightings & Prayers

How else has God revealed himself to you this week? What do you think God wants you to do in response? Jot down some thoughts here. Then, when you've zeroed in on an action you feel God is prompting you to take, use a dry-erase marker to write it on your bedroom or bathroom mirror.

"I'm reading not to get through, but to see God, in the readings each day and from what others share weekly. That, to me, is the real cause for celebration! I was nervous to begin, wondering if/when/how I would see God, but I am! And it's now not just through the day's reading, but from what I have read before and how this is spilling into the rest of my life. I'm more watchful to see what God is showing me."

—Deb Bernard, product manager

God Sightings

Commitment. Total dedication. Giving your entire self. That's the passionate response God's looking for from you.

This week, look for people who are giving their all to something or someone. The jogger who burns up the last hundred yards in a sprint. The student who won't settle for 100 percent but has to nail the bonus question, too. The couple who are still madly in love…50 years after their wedding day. Keep a list in your journal.

Each time you see commitment, let it remind you: That's how God feels about you. And wants you to feel about him. It's a God Sighting.

Reflection Questions

What particular passage of Scripture really jumped out at you like a glaring neon sign, flashing into your life this week? What was its message to you?

God is at work in all your relationships. What's one specific relationship with a loved one, a friend, or even a difficult person in which you've recently seen God move? Describe what God has been up to.

Sometimes God shows up "in disguise"—in ways we don't recognize at first. God might use an annoying co-worker to refine your own character, or he might encourage you through the kind action of a stranger. What disguise did God wear in your life this past week? Did you recognize God at the time? Why or why not?

❧WEEK 5—January 29–February 4

Exodus 8:1–21:21; Matthew 19:13–23:39;
Psalms 24–28; Proverbs 6:1–7:5

How has God's deep, wide, and amazing love for you broken through your everyday routine this week? How do you want to respond? Doodle a heart below, and write in it a simple statement declaring what you'll do this week to show God how much you love him.

"I stumbled onto the Old Testament passage [Exodus 18] in which Jethro pays a visit to his overworked son-in-law, Moses...The next day, I met with my agent and canceled my speaking engagements for the coming year. That led to my decision to videotape the final weekend seminar, which was eventually seen by eighty million people worldwide and led to the development of Focus on the Family. By giving priority to my family, as modeled in the conversation between Jethro and Moses, I embarked on an entirely new outreach to others."

—James C. Dobson, founder, Focus on the Family*

God Sightings

Serving others…how often this week will you do that?

A buck dropped in a beggar's cup. A midnight walk around the block with Fido, even if it's not your turn. Ten minutes you can't spare given to a colleague so he can tell you all about his vacation.

Small kindnesses. Small gifts of service.

They're really not so small, you know. Because when you serve others, you're serving God as well.

This week, keep track of services you provide—and receive—here in your journal. They're God Sightings.

Reflection Questions

What has God revealed to you about yourself in your reading of Scripture this week?

How has God given you an opportunity to love him by loving others this week? How did you respond?

Sometimes, like an old-fashioned radio, we need to get our lives "in tune" and clear out the static in order to hear God clearly. What have you done this week to tune in to God?

How is God calling you to hit the pavement—to put action and effort behind your desire to know him and follow him? Sketch some walking feet in the space below to show your desire to take action. Near your drawing, write one specific step you'll take this week to follow God's leading in your life.

God Sightings

Ever wonder what God has in mind for you and your life? You know—*specifically?*

Start in God's Word.

Whatever you think God may have in mind for you—whether it's starting an orphanage, moving to Minnesota, or giving up accounting to write that novel—the Bible provides rock-solid direction.

This week, jot a note each time you see an opening to follow God's direction…and note how you responded to the opportunity.

The openings you saw were God Sightings…but did you respond?

Reflection Questions

Jesus called his disciples to follow him (see Mark 1:17 and 2:14). In what specific ways has God been challenging you through his Word to follow him?

How has God used someone as a Christ-like example to inspire you in your own spiritual walk this week?

Psalm 34:4 says, "I prayed to the Lord, and he answered me. He freed me from all my fears." What fears has God freed you from this week? What darkness has he led you through? What confusion has he helped you see beyond?

❧ WEEK 7—February 12-18

Exodus 34:1–Leviticus 7:27; Matthew 27:15–Mark 3:30; Psalms 33:12–37:11; Proverbs 9:1–10:4

More God Sightings & Prayers

How else has God been working behind the scenes in your life? In what ways is Jesus saying, "Follow me: Live like me, love like me, show me to the world"? Write your answer to Jesus' call here as if you're writing him a letter—be sure to tell him what specific choice you'll make or action you'll take to be more like him.

"Often falling asleep with the Bible open across my chest, I wondered how God could use my broken life. One day I came across Psalm 34:18. The love Jesus had for broken people became the lifeline that saved me... From my personal brokenness, I can now speak to others who feel lost and hopeless."

—Bonnie Keen, songwriter and member of First Call*

God Sightings

Given how much waiting we do, you'd think we'd be more patient. We get to practice waiting in lines…in traffic…for phone calls to be returned.

This week, keep track of where you find yourself waiting…and why. Make a note here in your journal.

But instead of complaining, do something with the time. While in line, pray for the people in front of you. While in traffic, pray for the people behind you. And ask yourself, What in my life is most worth waiting for? What's the point of patience?

This week, lines aren't a burden. They're God Sightings.

Reflection Questions

How has God spoken to you through your readings this week? Did he show you anything unexpected?

In what other ways has God spoken to you this week? What people or situations has he used to show himself to you?

If you could ask God for one message in the sky— written in the clouds by a skywriter—what would it be about?

More God Sightings & Prayers

Write down what God's been showing you this week. Write what you've seen in the form of a prayer, thanking God for showing himself to you and asking how he wants you to respond.

God Sightings

This week, watch for children's enthusiasm for diving into new things, their willingness to believe in things they can't see, and their trust in those they love.

Childlike: embracing life with an open heart.

How open are you to trusting God? to his communicating his love in surprising ways? How childlike are you willing to be?

This week, consider each opportunity to trust—and each surprise—a God Sighting. Describe your God Sightings here. How is God calling you to embrace life with an open heart?

Reflection Questions

What struck you about what you read in God's Word this week? What do you think that might mean for you?

What's been going on in your life this week? How have you seen God at work in the midst of it?

Have you noticed any particular way or place that you most often spot God?

❧WEEK 9—February 26–March 4

Leviticus 19–Numbers 3; Mark 8:11–12:17;
Psalms 42–47; Proverbs 10:17-25

More God Sightings & Prayers

Keep it simple. What has God shown you this week? What do you suppose he wants you to do about it? Write it down. Then do it.

God Sightings

It's one thing to feel it and another to keep it.

And while it's rare, you'll see it if you look: joy.

It's the laughter you hear as you pass a playground. The light in the eyes of a co-worker who has just been praised. Anyone thanked sincerely for a job well done. Spikes of joy, flashes of happiness.

This week, describe the joy you see. What prompts it? What keeps it burning in the hearts of those around you? What keeps it burning in *your* heart?

See joy for what it is: a God Sighting.

Reflection Questions

How did God's Word nudge you this week? Why do you think God touched you that way?

How are you feeling God's touch in other parts of your life this week?

Is there anything you'd like God to speak to you more clearly about? Describe it here.

❧ WEEK 10—March 5-11

Numbers 4:1–16:40; Mark 12:18–15:47;
Psalms 48–54; Proverbs 10:26–11:6

More God Sightings *& Prayers*

If God were to hit you over the head, so to speak, would you recognize him? Think about the past few weeks. Does a pattern emerge? Write your observations and what you think God might want you to do about what he's been saying to you.

"In the book of Numbers, the Israelites time and time again went to Moses and complained that they wanted to go back to Egypt. Their trust in God was always in question. It was laughable, if not almost annoying, how many times they complained. As we read those complaints over and over, we started to wonder, What in our lives do we question over and over again? My husband reminded me that I have been worried about money for the 30 years he has known me. It hit me that I, like the Israelites, have trust issues. Now it is my turn to stop complaining and start trusting."

—Sheila Halasz, Christian preschool director

God Sightings

Where do *you* see God's creativity and power?

In the faces of your family? In the stars shimmering overhead? In the potted plant on your co-worker's desk?

This week, keep an eye out for anything that reminds you of God's greatness. His glory. Make a note of those things here.

God's glory isn't limited to the huge stuff. To mountains, meadows, and the Milky Way. Look for him working in and through the small things, too—the stuff of daily life.

They're all God Sightings.

Reflection Questions

What do you think God's been telling you through his Word? Does his message seem clear or muddled?

How has God been working through other people in your life? Can you see him at work in any particular situations?

Has God been faithful to answer any prayers or fulfill any promises in the past week? Watch for subtle blessings as well as obvious ones.

More God Sightings & Prayers

How has God been communicating with you? Does God seem to have been whispering? giving you a gentle hug? trying more forcefully to get your attention? List all the ways God's been faithful to you. Then thank God for everything on your list!

"During a particularly difficult time at work, it seemed as if I could do nothing right…My perception was that no matter what I did or how hard I tried, the politics of the workplace were predestined to end my twenty-five-year career and leave me with nothing…Psalm 138 reminded me to trust God's plans for me, and it brought assurance that ultimately that plan would be made clear, even if I could not discern it now in the midst of the overwhelming issues."

—Steve Sexton, manager of remittance processing for a national organization*

Week 12

Words From the Heart

God Sightings

This week, listen carefully to the words around you. The hurtful words. The healing ones. Listen for the heart behind those words.

And pay special attention to your *own* words.

Quote yourself here, in your journal. Are the words you toss out to friends and co-workers words of encouragement and peace? the soundtrack of a heart fueled by love of God?

Or something else?

This week, *listen* for God Sightings...for words of grace.

Reflection Questions

How did God catch your attention through his Word this week?

How have you seen God working through other people this week? What has he shown you in the workings of your life?

What's the most unusual way God spoke to you this week? What do you think he was telling you through this experience?

What else has God shown you this week? Write a letter to God about what he's been revealing to you.

"I began to contemplate the many empty relationships I had built with family and friends, when God brought to mind the opening words of the Sermon on the Mount. That first beatitude had always left me wondering to whom Jesus was referring when he talked about 'the poor in spirit.' In that moment, God opened my eyes to the unseen realm. It was me. I was among the poorest of the poor, totally dependent on the King...In that newfound humility, I yielded control to him and found myself a changed person."

—Janell Price, writer and editor*

God Sightings

Maybe you're not a big fan of rules. Every time a car chirps to remind you to fasten a seat belt, you secretly wish the government would just leave you alone.

But consider what's behind seat belts and speed limits. Most rules exist to protect someone or something. They're guardrails to keep you safe.

This week, list rules here in your journal as you bump up against them. Let them remind you of God's rules in your life—and why they're there. How they help you have a growing friendship with a loving and holy God.

Consider them God Sightings.

Reflection Questions

How have you listened closely and heard God's voice this week? How have you obeyed him?

What has reminded you to fear and obey the Lord throughout this week?

What miraculous signs and wonders would you like to see God do in your life? How do you think that would affect your willingness to listen and obey?

❧WEEK 13—March 26–April 1

Deuteronomy 5–20; Luke 7:11–9:50;
Psalms 68:19–73:28; Proverbs 11:29–12:10

More God Sightings & *Prayers*

List things you've heard from God this week. Next to that list, list how you've listened and obeyed. Write or draw a prayer, a conversation between you and God. Include confession of sin, thanksgiving for your relationship, and any requests you have.

"I discovered Psalm 71:14. I remember starting at that verse and thinking, I can't change my circumstance. I can't change my husband. I can't change our health. But I can change how I think about all of these things. I can choose hope, even if I don't feel hopeful. I can decide to believe that life will get better no matter how bad it looks now. I can choose to trust God despite what I see, and I can decide ahead of time that when I am most afraid, that's when I will praise God more."

—Claudine Stubbs Henry, author and director, Heartstring Ministries*

Week 14
Go Ahead—Ask

God Sightings

Confession time: Maybe you've wondered if this God Sightings thing is a bit… lame. Yes, you see God working—but only indirectly. If God's so powerful, shouldn't his work be a little more noticeable?

This week, ask God to *do* something. Something specific. Something consistent with what he's about in the world.

Here in your journal, keep track of what you ask. Then watch for doors to open, for possibilities to be revealed, for opportunities to arise.

As God answers your prayers, see those answers for what they are. They're God Sightings.

Reflection Questions

In your reading, how did you notice God asking you to change or grow?

In what other ways did you notice God at work in your life this week?

What do you most often ask God for? Are there other things God might want you to ask him for? If so, what?

More God Sightings & Prayers

What prayer requests have you brought to God this week? What answers have you gotten? What else would you like to bring before God? Make this the beginning of a prayer journal; note how God answers your prayers.

"Little did I know how important our family verse, Deuteronomy 31:8, would become…Six years after our wedding, my first husband died in an automobile accident…I remember, one particular night, reaching my hands to heaven and calling out to God, 'Lord, I need you! I feel so alone!'…With tears streaming down my face, I began to quote his Word. What was the first verse that came to mind? Deuteronomy 31:8. When my emotions threaten to take control, the stability of that Scripture verse keeps me grounded."

—Susan Kelly Skitt, speaker and mentoring specialist*

God Sightings

Especially in tough times, we're keenly aware of our finances. We think about money, dwell on it, try to find security in it.

Which means we're looking in exactly the wrong spot.

Every time you pay for something this week, pause. Don't let go of your money without a quick prayer: "God, help me trust you more than this green stuff."

What changes? Keep track here in your journal.

And that shift you feel within you? That's a God Sighting.

Reflection Questions

How did you notice God seeking you through his Word this week?

In what other ways did you sense God pursuing you?

How does knowing that all-powerful God loves and pursues you make you feel? How does that knowledge affect your relationship with God?

↬WEEK 15—April 9-15

Deuteronomy 33:1–Joshua 12:24; Luke 13–17;
Psalms 78:65–84:12; Proverbs 12:25–13:6

More God Sightings & Prayers

Throughout this week, notice the times and places you see God. Write or draw those occasions here. At the end of the week, look at what you wrote or drew. Do you notice any patterns? For example, do you sense God more when you're outdoors, with people, or pursuing a hobby?

God Sightings

This week, record what you see as you watch people. And watch them with this in mind: *What—or who—do people in your life serve?*

Catch hints in snatches of conversation. Listen to the stories that co-workers, family members, and friends tell. Watch for answers in their eyes. Who's *really* in charge in the lives of people you know?

Pray for people who seem to be ruled by "little g" gods such as money, ego, or fear.

Celebrate the people whose lives reflect faith. Hope. Love. Those lives are God Sightings.

Reflection Questions

What have you read this week about your relationship with God—what it means, what it looks like, what God wants?

Where have you noticed your relationship with God being stretched this week?

What else do you think God would like to say to you about your relationship with him?

❧ WEEK 16—April 16-22

Joshua 13–24; Luke 18:1–21:28; Psalms 85–89; Proverbs 13:7-23

More God Sightings *& Prayers*

Draw a picture that shows your relationship with God as a tree. What kind of tree is it? How is it growing or blossoming? What new growth has God produced in you through your God Sightings this week? What could you do to cultivate your tree to make it grow taller and stronger? Talk with God as you draw.

"When I'm really searching and seeking, God sometimes speaks to me in the night. More than once I've had a vivid dream from the Lord. He always awakens me when it is over and still fresh in my mind. I ask him to let me know if the dream came from him, and he does. For that reason, I keep a notebook and lighted pen (so I won't wake my husband) on the headboard of the bed."

—Lena Nelson Dooley, author, editor, and speaker*

God Sightings

First, a quick reminder: Jesus is God's Son. Savior. King. You don't get much more important than that.

But in a garden, dreading the task of carrying the world's sin, Jesus asked to be spared. Still, he was willing to do what God wanted—no matter what. That dedication took him to the cross.

Doing what needs to be done—no matter what. Look for people who are doing just that this week. The colleague who guts out a project and hits her deadline. The postal worker slogging through foul weather. The one in your family who makes sure food is on the table. Who's doing what needs to be done?

Describe those dedicated people here. Pray for them. And ask, What is God calling me to do this week—no matter what?

Reflection Questions

What has God drawn your attention to in his Word this week?

How have you kept yourself alert toward God in other areas of life?

In general, do you notice yourself more aware of God when times are good or when they're hard? Where are you right now?

More God Sightings *& Prayers*

Write a letter to God to tell him how you feel about your life and faith. After every few sentences, pause to listen for God's response. Use a different color pen to record what you hear. Continue the dialogue throughout the week.

God Sightings

Ever wonder what God's up to these days? Here it is: He's in the rescue business. It's why Jesus came and why Jesus died. And as long as anyone walking through your life today lacks a friendship with God through Jesus, it's a mission not yet accomplished.

This week, cooperate with God's work in the world.

Jot down the names of friends and acquaintances who don't have a friendship with God. Pray for those people. Be open to sharing your faith story with them.

This week, don't just look for God Sightings. Become one.

Reflection Questions

Think of the different characters you encountered in Scripture this week. Which ones do you think were easier for God to love? Which ones do you think were harder for God to love? Why?

Think of the characters in *your* story. Which ones present the greatest challenge when it comes to loving them? Why is that?

Sometimes it's easier to imagine God loving the world than it is to imagine him loving certain individuals, or even yourself. Why do you think that is?

More God Sightings *& Prayers*

Each day choose someone different in your circle—maybe a
family member, co-worker, or relative—and insert his or her
name into this prayer:

"God, you so loved _____ that you sent your only Son.
Please help me to see this person as you do, to the point that I
imitate your love toward _____. Amen."

"God, you so loved _____ that you sent your only Son.
Please help me to see this person as you do, to the point that I
imitate your love toward _____. Amen."

"God, you so loved _____ that you sent your only Son.
Please help me to see this person as you do, to the point that I
imitate your love toward _____. Amen."

"God, you so loved _____ that you sent your only Son.
Please help me to see this person as you do, to the point that I
imitate your love toward _____. Amen."

"God, you so loved _____ that you sent your only Son.
Please help me to see this person as you do, to the point that I
imitate your love toward _____. Amen."

"God, you so loved _____ that you sent your only Son.
Please help me to see this person as you do, to the point that I
imitate your love toward _____. Amen."

"God, you so loved _____ that you sent your only Son.
Please help me to see this person as you do, to the point that I
imitate your love toward _____. Amen."

God Sightings

Food...water...oxygen. You need them to live.

But God wants you to turn to *him* for what you need. To see him as your ultimate provider. That's where Jesus comes in. He's the bread of life.

This week, when you eat or drink, remember what Jesus said. Thank him for the food he's provided, and then ask him to fill you more deeply, in a lasting way. Jot down what you say—and what you hear in return.

Whatever you receive is a gift from God...a God Sighting.

Reflection Questions

One of the writers of Psalms invited his listeners to "taste and see that the Lord is good." Choose a few of the people you encountered in the Bible this week. How do you think God "tasted" to them?

Think of your recent encounters (or lack of encounters) with God. What words would you use to describe how God tastes to you? Sweet? Bitter? Like comfort food?

What appetites do you have that you wish God would satisfy? If God were to "cook up" a solution for you, how would it look? How would it taste?

How else did you connect with God in your reading? How can you bring God's "flavor" into your week? Write your thoughts in the form of a recipe:

God Sightings

Freedom comes in different sizes.

There's your ability to choose what to eat for dinner. Which TV shows to watch. What to wear tomorrow. Nice freedoms—but nothing special.

And then there's *significant* freedom…freedom you can't attain on your own. Like freedom from sin—a freedom that comes only through Jesus.

This week, notice your freedoms, the times you get to make choices. Let each choice be a reminder: There's a freedom that's deeper. Rarer. Far more valuable.

It's the freedom you can experience only in Jesus.

What will you do with that freedom this week?

Reflection Questions

What people in your reading seemed to live their lives with the most freedom and independence? Whose destinies seemed to be controlled by others?

As you've encountered God this week, did you feel your freedom expanding or contracting? Why?

What enslaves you? If God were to show up and rescue you, what would he do? What would he ask you to do?

✢WEEK 20—May 14-20

1 Samuel 15–28; John 8:1–11:54;
Psalms 110–117; Proverbs 15:8-23

More God Sightings *&* *Prayers*

So what else is God teaching you this week? Use the space below to design an icon that would help you remember that lesson.

God Sightings

This week, look for connections. An elderly couple taking a stroll. A mother clutching her child's hand as they cross a busy street. You exchanging a laugh with a friend.

Jesus wants to be connected to you. He wants a friendship with you that enables you to live a God-pleasing life. One that's rich, full, and fruitful.

Capture connections here in your journal this week. Connections between you and others. Between you and God.

They're more than heart-warming. They're God Sightings.

Reflection Questions

If your connection to God through the Word were like a hose, how would you describe it? Kinked? Leaky? Full? Why?

What are some other ways you noticed your connection to God this week?

What about God provides you with the most nourishment? What do you need God to supply more of? Why?

Write "God" on the left side of the page. Draw a picture of yourself on the right. Now illustrate the ways you stay connected to God. What does God supply? What do you take responsibility for?

"My mother was dying…God impressed on me the fact that the first three verses of John 14 were for my mother. I was desperate to be there with her, desperate to share these with her, but it was not to be. A few days after my mother's passing, my brother asked me to choose the Scripture for the memorial card, and I selected John 14. Although I had talked to my mother about salvation and had prayed for her, I was not sure whether she had made a commitment to Christ…When the service was over, my stepsister called me to her side and said, 'I just have to tell you—those verses you chose?—I read them to your mom right before she died.' God sent someone else to do what I could not do and was gracious enough to share it with me."

—Julie Momyer, teacher and researcher*

God Sightings

Willing to take a dare? Good! Pull off your shoes, close your eyes, and walk briskly across the room.

Light helps, doesn't it?

When there's light on your path, your toes relax. You know where you're going. You avoid problems.

This week, each time you flick on a light switch, thank God for shining light onto your path. Each time illumination floods the room, it's a God Sighting.

Note the times God helps light your way this week. They're God Sightings.

Reflection Questions

Where did God "turn on the lamp" for you in your readings this week?

How did God brighten your path as you navigated your daily life?

What "lamp on" moments did you experience? When did it feel as if you were moving along in the dark?

WEEK 22—May 28–June 3

2 Samuel 13–21; John 17–Acts 1;
Psalms 119:81–121:8; Proverbs 16:6-18

More God Sightings & Prayers

To shed a different light on your God Sightings, turn off all the lights in your place. As you turn each light back on, stop to pray for insight into the way God guided your path this week. Then make a list of all the "light moments" you recalled.

"I was sitting next to my husband in a quiet hospital room. He had been in severe pain for four very long days. I began to quietly play some familiar praise music, hoping to soothe him into rest. It seemed to work, and I thought he'd finally fallen asleep…when I heard him softly mumble in his semiconsciousness, 'I will lift my eyes to the Healer of the hurt I hold inside; I will lift my eyes to You.' He was singing along with a song by Bebo Norman. Though my husband wasn't really awake, the Spirit living in him was worshipping his Creator and Healer, and I knew it would be alright."

—Stephanie Caro, speaker and writer

God Sightings

Ever feel that, no matter how hard you try, you're doomed to fall short? Some weeks are like that.

But if you're doing God's will, you're a success. No matter what the results. No matter where the chips fall.

This week, look for people beating the odds. List them here. People who soldier on no matter what, who live life with a purpose. Let them remind you you're not alone. They're God Sightings in your week.

Because mountain moving isn't about you—it's about God.

Reflection Questions

How did you experience God's power working in yo through this week's readings?

When and how did you see that power at work in th world around you?

What situations did you bump up against this week that you handled all by yourself? If you had tapped into God's power, how would the results have been different?

More God Sightings & Prayers

When faced with a tough situation, where do you turn for help, power, or consolation? Make a list, and be as complete and honest as possible. If it's alcohol, chocolate, or pills, list it. Which choices are healthy? Which aren't? How can you rely on God's power instead? Ask God to reveal an action plan for seeking and seeing his power in your life.

"After the robbery I refused to turn off the lamp beside my bed at night whenever my husband was away. Sleep evaded me, and caring for my children the next morning became a major burden. Finally, in desperation, I cried to God for deliverance from my fear. He spoke to me through Psalm 127:1, and I came to a new understanding of God's plan for provision and protection."

—Grace Fox, speaker and writer*

God Sightings

Keep this journal handy this week—you're on the lookout for harmony. Unity

Co-workers cooperating. A family sharing a picnic in the park. Friends playing basketball. People enjoying people, sharing life together.

Write down what you see and hear.

Harmony is music to God's ears. Harmony in nature, harmony in relationships.

Harmony is love in action. It's a God Sighting.

Reflection Questions

Reflect on this week's readings, especially Psalm 133:1-2. As you read, what harmony did you sense from reading God's words?

As you traveled through your week, what measure of the harmony this passage describes, if any, did you experience? Why or why not?

Reflect on a moment this week when you felt someone or something bringing harmony or unity to your life.

❧ WEEK 24—June 11-17

1 Kings 8–18; Acts 7:51–11:30;
Psalms 129–135; Proverbs 17:1-13

More God Sightings & Prayers

What has God shown you about harmony this week? How can your life be in greater harmony with those around you and with God?

God Sightings

If your life feels crowded, here's why: There are billions of people in the world…and most of them are ahead of you in line at Starbucks.

Yet every person is also a unique work of art. God made each person—just as he carefully crafted you.

This week, take note of the people in your life. Who they are. How they're wired. What makes them tick. They're God Sightings, examples of God's creativity and imagination.

List the good things you see in people you love. Thank God for his wonderful workmanship.

Reflection Questions

As you read God's Word this week, what did God bring to mind about yourself?

How did God show you your worth to him as you went about your week?

If you were to change anything about yourself, what would it be? Why? What do you imagine God's response to that desired change would be?

❧Week 25—June 18-24

1 Kings 19–2 Kings 7; Acts 12:1–16:15;
Psalms 136–142; Proverbs 17:14-25

Look at yourself in the mirror. Slowly read Psalm 139:13-14 aloud. Look at your image again. Write a prayer, thanking God for the marvelous workmanship reflected in you.

God Sightings

Set a chair by a window.

Notice the shadow. Check it now and then. See how it moves throughout the day—and fades as the light dies.

We seldom consider shadows, seldom think anything of them. But human life is like that shadow—brief and easily overlooked.

Except by God—who sees you. Loves you. Keeps you.

This week, let shadows be God Sightings. Write your thoughts as you consider how fragile shadows are…and how powerful God's love for you is.

Reflection Questions

How did God reveal more about himself in his Word this week?

As you went through the past week, where did you see God at work around you?

Zoom in on today: If your day were measured by a speedometer, how fast were you going? How much time did you carve out for this reflection?

❧WEEK 26—June 25–July 1

2 Kings 8–19; Acts 16:16–21:17;
Psalms 143–149; Proverbs 17:26–18:8

Read Psalm 144:3-4 three times. Pause between each reading to simply be still. Empty your mind. No thinking, speaking, praying, or writing. After the third reading and quiet moment, write down what God is saying to you.

God Sightings

Your mother was right: The company you keep defines you. At least it defines you to anyone *looking*.

This week, jot down the names of your companions here in your journal. Who's in your circle? How do they behave? What do they believe? In what ways are they God Sightings…drawing your attention back to God?

And what's their impact on you?

What was good advice when you were 10 is still good advice: Select your friends carefully. Prayerfully.

Are you heeding it?

Reflection Questions

What advice from God did you glean from this week's readings?

Where did you see God at work around you? What guidance did you receive from watching God at work?

Think of all the ways, other than turning to God, that people seek advice. When have you done the same, and how did it work out for you?

❧WEEK 27—July 2-8

2 Kings 20–1 Chronicles 6; Acts 21:18–26:32; Psalm 150; 1–6; Proverbs 18:9-21

More God Sightings & Prayers

What's the best advice God has ever given you? How did it come about? How has it influenced your life? Write about it here.

God Sightings

This week is all about your senses—using them to soak in God's creation around you.

The color of the sky. The scent of a flower. The sharp tang of orange juice on your tongue. The sound of a child laughing. The warmth of a friend's hand.

Every sense pulls God's power and divinity into sharper focus...if you'll let it.

All of creation is a God Sighting. Let it flow across you and—through you—into your journal.

Write a love note to God. Thank him for his creation.

Reflection Questions

How did God speak to you this week through his creation? How did it affect your week?

Where was God's power at work in your life this week? How did you respond?

How far would God have to go to reveal himself to you this week? What act of nature would bring you closer to him?

More God Sightings & Prayers

Each day this week, use this space to jot down things you see in nature that speak to you about God.

"When I was in college, I accepted a bet to prove that Christianity was a lie and that most Christians had pretty much lost their brains…A few years later…I became known as the guy who would share his faith with anybody at any time—strangers, addicts, and especially youth. In my first week in organized ministry, I typed Romans 1:16 on a card and hung it over my desk. When you know the power source, you really have no choice but to be bold!"

—Josh McDowell, speaker, apologist, and author*

God Sightings

Think about what you do to earn a living. How you go about getting dollars, grades, or affirmation.

Do you receive what you deserve for your efforts?

This week, watch for times you feel slighted, and then record those times here, in your journal. When do you wish you would get what you deserve? And how much would be enough?

A hard truth: *You don't want what you deserve.* Not really. Not from God and, maybe, not from others.

That you receive grace instead is the ultimate God Sighting.

Reflection Questions

What is the best gift God has given you this week? in your life? What does this gift tell you about God?

What areas of your life need assurance right now? How can God speak into these areas?

What do you need to know from God right now? How will you know that you've heard from God?

More God Sightings & Prayers

Draw a line in the space below. On the left side of the line, write, "Apart from God." On the right side, write, "Close to God." Mark an X to indicate where you are right now in your relationship with God. What would it take to move you closer to God? What promise does God give you through this week's Scripture to help you move forward?

God Sightings

So—who owns you? Or more to the point, to whom have you given yourself?

Who or what commands your attention, time, and money? Who or what do you drop everything for? Your job? Your spouse? Your Internet server?

This week, watch for times you snap to attention. Jot them in your journal. Odds are good you've given lots of people and things your loyalty…but are they worthy?

Let those snap-to-attention moments be reminders of who best deserves your loyalty and love: God. Let the rest of the distractions be reminders—God Sightings.

Reflection Questions

What has refreshed you this week through the readings?

Where in your life have you experienced something that was good and pleasing and perfect? What does this reveal to you about God?

What area of your life may God want to renew? How can he help you through the process of change?

More God Sightings & Prayers

How is God working in your life right now? What do you think God wants to change in you so you will be renewed? Write an action step you think God desires for your life this week.

"The ministry asked me to consider shifting to the Customer Service Department. I struggled with the image of leaving my private office, computer, and desk to move to a little cubby down the hall. I asked God, 'Do you want me to answer phones?' In response, he directed me to Romans 12:16, asking if I was willing to humble myself…And you know what? For that season, for that ministry, for my own good, and for God's glory, that was exactly where I was supposed to be."

—Sue Cameron, speaker and writer*

God Sightings

Look for dying people this week.

Not by dropping into a hospice facility for a bed-to-bed inspection. Rather, stay on the lookout for people choosing to live without God.

There's life in Jesus...but he doesn't force anyone into a friendship with him. Which means some people around you are choosing to live without life—an odd choice.

Jot in your journal the names of people who seem lifeless. Pray for them. Consider them God Sightings...reminders of God's empowering love.

Reflection Questions

Where is God asking you to follow him? What might happen if you do? How do you feel about following?

When this week did you get clear direction from God? How did you figure out what God wanted you to do, and how did you respond?

What's your first reaction to the word *obey*? Why? What about *repentance*? What role might God want obedience and repentance to play in your life, and why? What's your reaction?

More God Sightings & Prayers

What one big thing is God leading you to do? What's one small thing? Write a description of each below, and include your thoughts and feelings…especially what you hope will come of whatever God is leading you to do.

God Sightings

Where do you feel safe these days? Snuggled deep in bed? Wrapped in a warm sweater? Sitting next to someone special?

Describe those places in your journal. Make a note each time you escape to a special hiding place, a place of protection.

Those spots are God Sightings, echoes of an even safer place where you will find yourself warmed…loved…and welcomed.

And that's in your friendship with God. So snuggle close to God. Let him be your safe place.

Reflection Questions

If you think God does offer you some kind of help and protection, how would you describe it?

What happened this week to help you discover, or rediscover, something about God?

How easy or difficult is it for you to find God in times of trouble or hurt, and why?

❧Week 32—August 6-12
Ezra 3:1–Nehemiah 5:13; 1 Corinthians 2:6–7:40; Psalms 28–32; Proverbs 20:24–21:7

What questions do you have about prayer? Write them below. Then
jot down thoughts and responses for each as you run across God's
answers through Scripture, other people, and times with God.

God Sightings

You know the feeling…and it's infuriating.

You meant to pass by that muffin, but here it is in your hand. The website you vowed to never again visit calls to you as if it had a voice. Temptation weaves its spell…and once again you're back where you started.

Write down what tempts you this week. Name those things…or people. Put them in black and white. And then invite God to work on your list.

Accept God's empowering mercy and grace—and let what once owned you slip into its proper place as a God Sighting. A reminder to take God at his Word.

Reflection Questions

How would you describe what it means to turn to God for help? for justice? for forgiveness? What else?

Where are you catching glimpses of God's love and faithfulness this week?

If you could be "rescued" in one way right now, what form would that rescue take? What do you think God might want you to know about this situation? about yourself? about him?

More God Sightings & Prayers

Think about the details of your life. Draw a box below. Now
consider: In what ways are you depending on God? Write these
inside the box. In what ways are you *not* depending on God?
Write these outside the box. Now consider how to move everything inside the box, into your relationship with God.

God Sightings

What reminders of death have you experienced this week? A cemetery you pass on the way to work? The obituaries you avoid reading in the daily paper? Word that an old friend is no longer in the world?

Whatever those reminders are, this week consider them God Sightings. Opportunities to turn the trick on death, to shout out a truth greater than the grave: Death no longer holds the last card. There's more.

Here in your journal, write a note to death. Remind it where it fits in the world. Powerful, yes.

But all powerful? Not where God's love rules.

Reflection Questions

What did this week's readings reveal to you about God's sovereignty, even in the worst of times?

In what ways has God reminded you of his presence, even in the midst of struggles, this week?

Think of the hardest thing you've ever experienced. How did God help you through that time?

More God Sightings & Prayers

What is your worst fear? Write it down. Then write a prayer to God, handing that fear over to him. Each time that fear arises in you, give it to God again. And again. Do this until you know God has truly lifted this fear from you.

God Sightings

Why would God pour his Spirit into something as fragile as we are? We break. We get hurt. We don't adequately reflect on our outside the good gift we hold inside.

But maybe that's the point: What we carry couldn't come from ourselves. We're just vessels.

This week, notice how the drinks you enjoy are served. Even sturdy mugs break. And carryout coffee cups? They define the word *fragile*.

Let cups, glasses, and mugs be God Sightings this week— ways of seeing God at work in the world. Of letting him remind you: You're a vessel of his glory.

Reflection Questions

What's the first word or phrase that comes to mind when you think of what God showed you through his Word this week? What does this word or phrase mean to you?

How has this word or idea popped up in unexpected places in your daily life? How has it challenged or encouraged you?

What's the first word that comes to mind when you think about God's character?

❧WEEK 35—August 27–September 2

Job 23–42 and Ecclesiastes 1–3; 2 Corinthians 1:12–6:13; Psalms 41–46; Proverbs 22:5-15

More God Sightings & Prayers

As you go about your daily life, remember the two words or phrases you thought of. Incorporate them into your daily prayers. Now write a prayer for the week. Center the prayer on those two words or phrases.

God Sightings

You're younger today than you'll be any other day for the rest of your life. So whatever your age—today you're young.

Look for young people this week—or at least the young at heart. How are they using their youth? Whom do they honor? Whom do they serve?

Journal your observations. Do their lives reflect God working in and through them? Are they God Sightings for those around them? places you see God at work?

And you? On this—the youngest of your remaining days—are *you* a God Sighting?

Reflection Questions

As you read the Bible this week, what did God reveal to you about what he wants for the rest of your life?

Has God pricked your conscience this week? Is there something you've been thinking or doing (or not doing) that God is bringing to your attention?

Imagine those little conscience pricks as pinches on the arm. Why do you think God sometimes "pinches" us like this? What does he want you to remember? What do you think God is trying to tell you?

❧WEEK 36—September 3-9

Ecclesiastes 4–Isaiah 5; 2 Corinthians 6:14–11:15; Psalms 47–53; Proverbs 22:16-29

Write about something negative in your life that you know God isn't satisfied with. Now cross that out, and write next to it what God wants you to remember and replace it with.

"I had been out of the Marine Corps for a year and had been divorced for two—all before I turned twenty-five. After receiving a call from my ex-wife, I broke down as I thought about our past and about what could have been. That's the night when God…broke through my stubbornness. He opened my eyes with Psalm 51:1-2…Until that moment, I had refused to admit that it was my own sinfulness that was causing my heartache… Within two years, my ex-wife and I remarried and have now been blessed with a precious little daughter."

—Joseph Beasley, worship leader*

God Sightings

This week, listen for Jesus' name. How it's used. Who uses it—and why. Keep track in your journal.

Just a guess: You won't often hear it used the way Jesus would prefer. Certainly not to describe how he's active in the world, what he's here to accomplish.

Also in your journal, list the descriptive names you find in Isaiah 9:6. Add your own descriptive names, each a recognition of what you see Jesus doing in your life, in his creation.

Each a God Sighting.

Reflection Questions

What one verse caught your attention this week, and why? What do you think God wants you to take away from it?

What happened this week to remind you of the mightiness of God?

Does the God you're reading about in the Old Testament seem to be the same God you experience in your everyday life? What questions are you left asking?

❧ WEEK 37—September 10-16

Isaiah 6–24; 2 Corinthians 11:16–Galatians 3:9; Psalms 54–60; Proverbs 23:1-16

More God Sightings & Prayers

As you go about your day, look for ways the God you're reading about in the Old Testament intersects with your own life. How can you see and experience that God is the same today as he was 30 years ago, 300 years ago, and 3,000 years ago? How does this change your perspective on God's involvement in your own life today? Write your thoughts and questions here.

"A car accident killed my father, paralyzed my mother, and forced my three siblings and me to leave home in Zambia and move to the overwhelming country of the United States...One night in college, when I was terribly down and was reading the Psalms, I discovered the verse that says, 'Oh, that I had wings like a dove; then I would fly away and rest!' I was stunned. Was it okay to want to fly away, to want to rest? I could not think of a thing I would rather do—but it seemed so unchristian somehow...Eventually I realized...it is okay to grieve for what is wrong in the world and to long for the world God created us for."

—Anna Joujan, librarian and cross-country coach*

God Sightings

This week is all about seeing God's character expressed in his world, in the lives of people in whom God lives.

Because that's part of the deal: Where God lives, you see him shaping character. You see consequences.

You see God Sightings...his impact and efforts.

In your journal, keep track of glimpses of God at work in the lives of others.

Where do you see God working in *you*? How is your friendship with God changing you?

Reflection Questions

What specific kinds of actions, behaviors, and attitudes do this week's readings indicate should be evident in your life if you're a Christian? What should not be part of your life?

What fruit of the Spirit do you think other people can see in your life, even if they don't know about your faith?

What fruit of the Spirit do you think God wants to develop in you?

More God Sightings & Prayers

Keep your eyes open for fruit of the Spirit in the Christians you know. Note what you see in the space below. And note ways these Christians have encouraged you and enriched your relationship with Jesus.

"As I hung up the phone, fear crept over me like a dark cloud. The doctors at UCLA had finally called with a date for my daughter's open-heart surgery…The next morning…I noticed a card on my desk from one of my room mothers. In bold letters on the front I read Isaiah 41:10…On the way home I turned on the radio just in time to hear the speaker quoting Isaiah 41:10…That night I called home…and poured out my doubt and fear to my stepmom. 'Honey, I want to read you what the pastor shared last Sunday'…As she read the words from Isaiah 41:10, I wept, knowing that God had gone to a great deal of trouble to let me know he was there for my daughter and me—now and forever."

—Linda Newton, educator, speaker, and counselor*

God Sightings

In a world of white lies, tweaked truth, and PR spins, you're stalking truth this week.

Where you find truth—especially truth told at a cost—you tend to find God hanging out. He's big on truth. He *is* truth.

Where do you see truth sacrificially told? honestly lived? softened by love, but still steel-spined and clear?

Those are God Sightings. Document them here. Pray for the people involved.

Become one of the people involved.

Reflection Questions

What did you read in the Bible this week that surprised you or really spoke to your heart?

How have you seen God use you this week through your unique role in the church body?

What blinds you to God Sightings? What could you do that would allow you to see God more clearly?

More God Sightings & Prayers

Write down the various roles God has given you. Next to each, write how you can use those roles to help those near you grow closer to Christ.

God Sightings

This week, look for people who are pushing on, forging ahead, intent on finishing what's ahead of them. Capture their stories in your journal.

Joggers. Bicyclists aiming for 20 miles. Co-workers intent on completing a task. People who refuse to let challenges keep them from reaching a goal.

They're not just inspirations. For you, this week, they're God Sightings. Reminders that living a faithful life doesn't require you to break the tape in a blaze of glory. You simply need to cross the finish line.

If you don't quit, you can't lose.

Reflection Questions

In what ways can you relate to the people in the passages you read this week?

What difficult circumstance are you having to push through?

How does God use difficult situations to reveal himself to you?

What does the finish line of the race you're running look like? Draw or write a description of the finish line. Now add a picture or description of where God is and what he's doing while you're pressing on through the race. What would help you to keep running? Talk to God about your race, and ask him to give you whatever you need to finish.

"Throughout high school, whenever I felt overwhelmed by academic and social pressures, my mom reminded me of what was quickly becoming 'my' verse. My parents inscribed Philippians 4:13 in my graduation Bible and gave me a plaque with it in big letters to remind me of this truth when I faced loneliness and the fear of failure at the university…Now I'm the mom. Our three sons will someday face fears of their own, and I know just the Bible verse to give them."

—Jeanette Armitage, full-time mom*

God Sightings

They're out there: people who do their jobs with a smile…and a positive attitude.

Maybe you're among them. Maybe not.

This week, ask positive people how they do it. How they sweep floors, sack groceries, or bind broken bones with such a positive attitude.

Write their answers in your journal. Compare what you hear with how you do what you do. With *your* attitude.

What's your motivation? your reward—beyond the paycheck? Are you a God Sighting?

Reflection Questions

What was the most personally significant thing you read in the Bible this week?

What revelation about your life have you had recently?

Who or what in your life most helps you see God Sightings? Why?

More God Sightings & Prayers

Make a conscious effort to look for God's presence in your work and daily routines. God is probably more present than you realize! Use the space below to record some of these God Sightings.

God Sightings

There's something about opening your front door and letting yourself in after a long, challenging day.

You're home. It's time to kick off your shoes and relax. You're someplace you belong.

Where do you feel most at home? This week, notice those places. Describe them in your journal.

Those places are God Sightings. Places God meets you with a blessing and an offer: Let's make this permanent. Come join the family. Come be my child.

Welcome home.

Reflection Questions

How have this week's readings shown you God's love and concern for you? his commitment to you?

How have you seen God take care of you this week, in both big and small ways?

What things have happened in your life that you initially attributed to coincidence, good luck, or being in the right place at the right time that you now attribute to God? Why?

❧WEEK 42—October 15-21

Jeremiah 26–38; 2 Thessalonians 3–
1 Timothy 6; Psalms 85–89; Proverbs 25:16-28

More God Sightings & Prayers

God has written his covenant with you on your heart and documented it in the Bible. Have you ever done something to make your relationship with God "official"? This week, think of a way of expressing your faith and your commitment to God. For example, you might write and sign a prayer, buy and wear a piece of Christian jewelry, or display something in your house that symbolizes that commitment. Whatever you choose, describe it here.

God Sightings

This week, look for written instructions that matter. Traffic signs. Warning labels on medicine bottles. The expiration date on that carton of milk.

You could ignore what you read…but why?

Your Bible is a God Sighting, a testimony to God's passion for reaching out to, for revealing himself. But reading is one thing. Taking what you read to heart and profiting from it is another.

In your journal, sum up what God tells you about himself this week through your Bible reading. What does he want you to know?

Reflection Questions

What did God show you in the other readings this week, aside from the key verse, 2 Timothy 3:16-17?

How has God surprised you this week?

How has God used a difficult circumstance in your life to teach you more about him?

More God Sightings & Prayers

How would your week have been different without God's influence and work in your life? Think of a way to thank God for his guidance during the past seven days. You could write a prayer, draw a picture, write a song or poem, take a picture, or even make a list of the ways you've seen him.

"My dad had been dying of cancer, and the entire family was gathered around his bedside as he was getting ready to leave this world to be with his Lord. We had thought he was leaving two nights earlier, but he kept hanging on. On the evening of October 19, my sister Pat was reading from Psalm 100. She read the entire psalm once, and then started it again. When she got to verse four, she paused. After a brief moment she quietly said, 'You may enter now.' With that, my dad took one last sighing breath, and we watched as he entered into God's gates."

—Nancy Foss, speaker and teacher*

God Sightings

This warm friendship with God...you're taking it seriously, right?

Because God's taking *you* seriously. And the truth you'll discover about yourself and him shines light into dark corners. It exposes you for who you really are.

What are you learning about yourself as you grow closer to God? What God Sightings do you have about God himself? Jot them here in your journal this week.

And thank God for the scalpel of his truth. For the healing it brings as we let ourselves be open before him.

Reflection Questions

How would you describe God's faithfulness? Write your definition in one sentence without using the word *faithful*.

What do you think God has been trying to say to you this week?

Why do you think God still pursues us, even when we're not actively seeking him?

More God Sightings & Prayers

What have you come to understand about God this week? How can you make sure you'll hold on to your new understanding? Think of the way you learn best, whether it's by music, words, socialization, or whatever. Then document your new insight that way—write a song, write a poem, tell a friend…you get the picture!

"Just before my twenty-seventh birthday, I experienced a miscarriage…I felt so empty that I didn't want to, but God somehow gave me strength to pick up his Word. I saw that my devotional reading for the day was in Lamentations. Not Lamentations! I thought. But as I began to read, I saw before my eyes the words of Lamentations 3:32-33. In that moment I literally felt God wrap me in his arms of love and comfort me as only he could."

—Cheryl Barker, writer and homemaker*

God Sightings

Here's the thing about God: He sees your heart. He has 20/20 insight into not just your *actions*, but also your *motives*. And guess which he cares about most?

God's all about heart…and what's in yours matters.

This week, be sensitive to moments you stiffen when asked to do something. When you want nothing more than to dig in your heels and shout, "No!" Notice the flashes of rebellion and pride that flit into view.

What you do with them is up to you. But that God is helping you see them for what they are? Those are God Sightings.

Reflection Questions

How has God been leading you this week?

In what ways has God used circumstances and other people to guide you this week?

In what area of your life do you need a change of direction right now? How willing are you to let God set the course for that new direction?

WEEK 45—November 5-11

Ezekiel 12–23; Hebrews 7–10;
Psalms 105:37–109:31; Proverbs 27:3-13

More God Sightings & Prayers

Draw a few arrows. This week, each time you see God leading you in his direction—not your own—write a response on one of the arrows. Maybe you'll thank God for his new direction, or maybe you'll tell him that you're scared to go there. However you feel, tell God about it!

"The third day I was at Maxwell Federal Prison Camp...I found an empty spot in the dayroom for some quiet Bible study and came across a verse that struck me hard: Christ has become human so that he would not be ashamed to call us his brothers (Hebrews 2:11)...I suddenly saw life differently. The men around me weren't 'murderers' and 'robbers' and 'drug dealers'; if Christ was not ashamed of them, they were brothers, human beings just like me."

—Charles W. Colson, author and founder, Prison Fellowship*

God Sightings

This week is all about what's real…but invisible.

Love, for instance. Confidence. Hope. Faith. Things that don't fit in a test tube but fuel our willingness to crawl out of bed in the morning. Invisible—but real.

This week, look for what you can't see with your eyes but trust with your heart. The unseen bridges between you and other people—and you and God.

Jot them down. Celebrate them. They're reminders that much of what God does in your world isn't visible—that some God Sightings are best seen with your heart.

Reflection Questions

What does the word *faith* mean to you in connection with God?

What's the difference between hope and faith? How is God showing you the difference?

How can you know whether what you hope for is in line with God's will for your life?

❧ WEEK 46—November 12-18

Ezekiel 24–38; Hebrews 11:1–James 2:17;
Psalms 110–117; Proverbs 27:14–28:1

More God Sightings & Prayers

Each morning this week, think of what you hope will happen that day. Be specific. Then filter out what you think is not in line with God's will. Watch as God works in your life this week, and see what he teaches you about faith and hope. Write down what you discover.

God Sightings

This week, listen for questions. They're God Sightings in disguise.

Questions about what—and why—you believe. Why you do what you do. Why you spend—or don't spend—money in certain ways, on certain things. Why you're bothering to read a Bible.

Listen carefully. Those questions are God Sightings, glimpses of God working to engage others and draw them closer to him…through you.

Share your story. Jot down the questions you hear. Pray for the questioners. And thank God that other people see something different in you, something that sparks questions.

Congratulations. To someone this week, *you're* the God Sighting.

Reflection Questions

From your readings, what do you think it means to make Jesus Lord of your life?

Think of one person you know who makes Jesus Lord of his or her life. What can you learn from that person?

Jesus *wants* to be Lord of your life; how is he teaching you what that means?

❧ WEEK 47—November 19-25

Ezekiel 39:1–Daniel 2:23; James 2:18–1 Peter 4:6; Psalms 118–119:80; Proverbs 28:2-14

More God Sightings & Prayers

A relationship with Jesus is like a relationship with a very best friend. What has Jesus, as your best friend, revealed about himself this week? How will you respond? What will you say to him? This week, keep a "best-friend diary," writing your thoughts and insights to Jesus as you would to your earthly best friend.

"Alone in my YMCA dorm room, I searched my Bible for direction—and cried myself to sleep, night after night. Late one night I came across a simple verse in Psalm 118 that seemed written just for me. 'This is the day the Lord has made. We will rejoice and be glad in it.'…I've returned time and time again to those few simple words. They always bring my focus back to where it should be: on him. This day. Rejoice!"

—Roxanne Henke, author*

God Sightings

Polite people look away. The ketchup stain on your friend's shirt? That smudge on the bank teller's collar? It's rude to point them out.

But this week, they're reminders: Some stains only God can remove. Some cleansing only he can provide.

In your journal, ask God to forgive your sin, your wrong choices, your failed behavior. Be specific—accept the humbling that comes with calling sin what it is.

Then erase what you've written. That blank space? That's a God Sighting…his work in action.

Reflection Questions

How have you learned to live more in God's light this week?

How has what you've read helped you have deeper fellowship with others this week?

In three words, how would you describe your response to how Jesus can cleanse us from sin?

Where in your house is the most light? Is it under the fluorescent light in the bathroom? at the table by the sunny kitchen window? Wherever it is, use that spot this week to document what you're learning about living in God's light.

God Sightings

Not everything God does is predictable. Comfortable. Something that fits into a regulation-size box.

This week, listen for God speaking in ways you haven't heard him speak before. Through people you wouldn't expect to be his spokespeople.

Jot down what you hear. Then ponder the messages. Do they sound like the God you know? Do they fit with what he's trying to accomplish? Is there a message for you in there?

Not all God Sightings are what you'd expect. But why should they be? They're from God.

Reflection Questions

What's the most unexpected thing you discovered about God through Scripture this week?

What or who revealed God to you in the most unexpected way this week?

How have your expectations of God limited your relationship with him?

❧Week 49—December 3-9

Daniel 11:2–Joel 3:21; 1 John 3:7–Revelation 1:20;
Psalms 122–128; Proverbs 29:1-18

More God Sightings & Prayers

God reveals himself to us in countless ways, yet often we forget what God has done to show us his love. Spend some time thinking about your life experiences, and then write a letter to your child or a dear friend describing how you've experienced God's great love for you.

"The death of my baby son, Timmy, began the Great Depression in my heart. I stopped caring—about my garden and my life. I gave in to the darkest parts of myself and wallowed, for months, in sorrow, anger, and self-pity…Then a friend gave me a card with the words of Hosea 10:12 written on it, and I made a tearful and painful decision to break up the hard places in my heart…As I began to reconnect with my friends and family, my garden and my life began to bloom again."

—Nancy C. Anderson, speaker and author*

God Sightings

Sharpen your pencil. This week, you'll note in your journal situations in which justice is done…mercy is shown…and others walk humbly with God.

Where are those things happening? Who's doing them—and why? You may be surprised. Not all who serve mankind serve God…yet God can use them.

Wherever you see justice done and mercy shown, be reminded of God's work in the world. They're God Sightings—his work done in the lives of the needy.

By the way—were you able to add your own name and work to your list?

Reflection Questions

What struck you about God's character as you read the Bible this week?

What aspect of God's character would you like to exhibit in your life?

What other "gods" have you pursued? Are you currently pursuing something other than God?

WEEK 50—December 10-16

Amos 1–Micah 7; Revelation 2–7;
Psalms 129–135; Proverbs 29:19–30:6

More God Sightings & Prayers

List at least five things you saw this week that made you think, *God, you are awesome.* Call a friend and share one of them.

God Sightings

A relationship explodes. Your finances implode. Your fan club shrinks to zero. You feel completely, achingly alone.

Except you're not. You're not alone. In the midst of whatever pain and self-doubt life tosses at you, you're not alone. There's a refuge waiting...if you'll go there.

This week, look for safe places. Traffic islands. Open blocks of time. Any unexpected oasis. Note what you find in your journal. And as you catch your breath in those places, thank God for being a refuge in dark times.

That calm you feel? It's a God Sighting.

Reflection Questions

How was God active in your life this week?

In what ways has God provided a safe haven for you during your lifetime?

How did God use you to help someone this week? What did you discover from that experience?

More God Sightings & Prayers

Memorizing Scripture not only helps us focus on what God is saying but also encourages us during difficult times. Choose a verse that stood out to you this week, and write it below. Commit this verse to memory, and see how God brings it to life in the weeks that follow.

"In the midst of corporate mergers and decisions of my own, I found myself jobless…Then, on a quiet morning, I heard it. I heard him. Jesus spoke to my heart, 'Be still, and know that I am God!' No screaming. No kicking. Just peace in his presence. It didn't take me long to realize that I had been missing everything of lasting significance…I now spend my days listening and praying to hear God's voice unceasingly. Day by day, his words are getting more distinct, more personal, and even more challenging."

—Michael Garrett, founder, Faith Cycle Ministries*

God Sightings

This week, note the places you find refreshment. Specifically, where you go to quench your thirst.

It could be a water fountain. A soda machine. A bottle of water after a long run.

Wherever it is, drink deep. Feel the liquid satisfy your thirst, feed your body, fuel your life. Feels great! But it's temporary…and God has something more lasting in mind for you.

Whenever you satisfy your thirst this week, pause to thank God for caring for your body. It's a God Sighting, a reminder of how much more he'll do for your soul.

Reflection Questions

Zechariah and Malachi both saw visions; God's voice was audible for them. How did God speak to you this week? What did God say?

How did you experience God's protection this week? Or maybe you experienced his mercy and grace. Write about it.

If you could praise God without inhibition, what would it look like? How would you like to express yourself in worship?

More God Sightings & Prayers

Take time to reflect on the God Sightings you've experienced throughout this journey. What have you learned about God? about yourself? Write a poem (don't worry about rhyming!) to God, praising him for his love, faithfulness, protection, or other attributes that have most touched you this year.

More God Sightings & Prayers